Catholics and Ecumenism

That All May Be One

Reverend Michael Parise

One Liguori Drive
Liguori, Missouri 63057-9999
(314) 464-2500

Imprimi Potest:
William A. Nugent, C.SS.R.
Provincial, St. Louis Province
The Redemptorists

Imprimatur:
Monsignor Maurice F. Byrne
Vice Chancellor, Archdiocese of St. Louis

ISBN 0-89243-303-5
Library of Congress Catalog Card Number: 89-83669

Copyright © 1989, Liguori Publications
Printed in U.S.A.

All rights reserved. No part of this book may be reproduced, stored in a retrieval system, or transmitted without the written permission of Liguori Publications.

Table of Contents

Introduction: New Hope for Christian Unity 5
1. Divisions and Separations in Christianity 8
2. Similarities and Differences Among Christians 17
3. Understanding the Many Christian Communities 24
4. Understanding Non-Christian Religions 38
5. Ecumenism — Healthy and Unhealthy 41
6. Ecumenism in Marriage and the Home 45
7. Ecumenism Among Family and Relatives 49
8. Ecumenism in the Parish 52
9. Ecumenism in the Community 57
Conclusion: That All May Be One 63

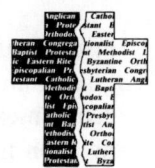

Introduction: New Hope for Christian Unity

The 1960s were a decade marked by great unrest and social upheaval: Assassinations, hippies, protests, racial violence, and the birth of the sexual revolution were indicative of just a few of the major cultural shifts that took place in North America. The decade of the sixties also signaled the start of a great period of change, growth, and rebirth in the Catholic Church. The actions of two thousand bishops gathered in Rome for the Second Vatican Council (1962-1965) initiated major shifts in the outlook and attitude of the Catholic Church, its leaders, and its faithful. These changes, far too numerous to list, affected every area of Catholic life and worship.

Efforts to seek greater harmony and achieve fuller union with other Christians and non-Christians indicate one of the major new directions adopted by the Catholic Church. Since the mid-sixties Catholics have taken many positive steps to improve relations with Christians who are not Catholics and with the members of non-Christian religions.

These efforts at greater understanding and unity are labeled as "ecumenism," a word derived from the Greek *oikoumene,* which means "universal" or "worldwide." Catholics did not invent ecumenism. For nearly a century many Protestant, Anglican, and Eastern Orthodox Christians have been engaged in ecumenical dialogue and action, trying to heal the wounds of division in the Body of Christ, the Christian community.

The ecumenical dialogues and discussions among many Protestant Churches have been formalized in the World Council of Churches, whose representatives are headquartered in Geneva, Switzerland. This organization aims to deepen cooperation, understanding, and unity among Christians, while acknowledging diversity in beliefs and practices. Without actually becoming a member of the World Council of Churches, the Catholic Church has followed closely the progress made within this organization.

The Second Vatican Council produced sixteen major documents which set forth the official teaching of the Catholic Church in such areas as the Church's understanding of divine revelation, the apostolate of the laity, religious liberty, missions, priestly ministry, and liturgy. Two of the written statements which emerged from the Second Vatican Council have provided the foundation for the ecumenical efforts of the Catholic Church since the mid-sixties. The *Decree on Ecumenism* offered theological and pastoral principles that encouraged and guided these new relationships between Roman Catholics and other Christians. The *Declaration on the Relation of the Church to Non-Christian Religions* announced a new and positive attitude toward non-Christians.

Henceforth, Catholics are no longer to consider other Christians as "schismatics" or "heretics." They are now spoken of as "separated brothers and sisters in Christ." The Catholic Church now acknowledges that the Holy Spirit — not the devil — is present in other Christian Churches. The Council documents also make it clear that while there are many religions, there is one God who wants all people to live together in love.

Since the Council, ancient condemnations between the pope and the patriarch of Constantinople have been lifted. Representatives of Anglican, Lutheran, Orthodox, and other Christian and non-Christian religions have entered into meaningful theological dialogue with high-ranking Catholic officials. Much agreement and understanding in the areas of Scripture, Baptism, the sacrificial nature of the Eucharist, ministry, and Church authority has been reached. Much more work needs to be done, however, before full unity can be realized.

This book offers Catholics the opportunity to review how the Body of Christ was splintered into many separate sects and denominations during its long history. It clearly presents those issues which unite Christians as brothers and sisters in the same Lord and those which remain stumbling blocks to complete reunion. It suggests many practical ways that Christians — individually, as couples and families, and in parishes and communities — can work together to find greater harmony and mutual benefit. Finally this book explains how Catholics can become more truly ecumenical and more sensitive to others' beliefs while remaining firmly convinced of the truth of the Catholic faith.

1.
Divisions and Separations in Christianity

The Unity of the Church

The Church, as Jesus Christ established it, has four *marks* or characteristics. As is professed in the Creed, the Church is to be one, holy, Catholic, and apostolic. It is to be undivided and eternal, free of discord and division. Jesus wants all his followers to be united in love with him and with his heavenly Father (see John 17:21). Jesus, the sole mediator between God and humankind, unifies the Church and all its members. Saint Paul speaks of Christ as the head of the Church and all the faithful as the members of Christ's Mystical Body (see 1 Corinthians 12:12-31). Through Baptism, the Holy Spirit of God dwells in each Christian, binding together all believers into the one, worldwide People of God.

Christ also intends the Church to be the visible sign of his continued presence on earth. The Church is empowered to complete the saving work which Christ inaugurated in his Passion, death, and Resurrection. The Church is also to serve as Christ's herald of glad tidings; to proclaim the Good News, the gospel of forgiveness and salvation.

This rather ideal view of the Church must be measured against the reality of the many Christian communities which form the Body of Christ today. The Bible, the basic beliefs of the Christian tradition, the celebration of Baptism and Eucharist, and the spiritual and moral teachings expressed in the New Testament offer a common ground for all Christian believers. History, culture, language, social and economic conditions, political events and personalities contribute to the diversity of the Church. Human imperfection and sinfulness lead to the painful divisions that divide and weaken the Church.

Early Problems of Belief

Throughout the history of the Church, well-meaning believers have, at times, interpreted Christ's message in a way that was not accepted by the rest of the Christian community or by its recognized leaders. After Christ's Ascension and the sending of the Holy Spirit at Pentecost, it took several centuries for the Church to make clear and explicit many of its basic beliefs. In the process of clarification, unacceptable teachings expounded by certain bishops and theologians took hold in various communities. These rival teachings sometimes led to *schism* or *heresy*. Schism is formally and willfully separating from the unity of the Church by refusing to accept all the central teachings of the Catholic Church. Heresy is the formal denial or doubt about one or more elements of the Catholic faith in a way which deliberately influences other people.

A large number of disagreements about the formulation of basic beliefs arose during the first centuries of the Church. Some of these died out quickly. Others developed and spread, then seemed to disappear, only to flare up again under different names. Some confused beliefs have continued to the present day under different forms or names.

One of the basic errors that arose in those early centuries involved the belief that there was a dualism between the spiritual and physical worlds; the body was evil while the spirit was good. Efforts to develop a clear and correct understanding of the Trinity brought clarity to some people and confusion to others. Further disagreements arose as Christians from different cultures struggled to explain the precise relationship between the divinity and humanity of Christ. Discussions about the nature and validity of the sacraments, the role of Mary as the Mother of God and the Mother of Christ, and the relative importance of free will and grace in the process of salvation led to other problems.

When confronted with these misunderstandings and the potential for division within the Church, the bishops met in councils to cut through the theological knots presented by opposing viewpoints. Searching the Scriptures and other early Christian writings, the council members formulated the Church's official teaching regarding God's revealed truth. The teachings that arose from these councils form the basic beliefs of the Christian religion. The teachings that Jesus Christ is true God and true man, that Mary is the Mother of God, that there are three coequal persons in the Blessed Trinity, and that salvation is a gift of God and not something that Christians earn by their own merit are just a few of the doctrinal formulations that arose from the early councils in response to divisions caused by theological disagreements. These statements of truth clarify what Christians ought to believe, and they maintain the integrity and unity of Catholic faith.

The Eastern Schism — 1054

During the first four centuries after Christ, the pope, as the bishop of Rome, gradually claimed pastoral authority over the whole Church. Bishops throughout the world looked to the pope for his leadership in condemning false teaching, settling theological disputes, and defending the populace from invading barbarian armies.

In the fourth century the Roman Emperor moved his capital from Rome to Constantinople (now called Istanbul in Turkey). As a result, the bishop or *patriarch* who resided in Constantinople gained prestige and authority, especially among the Christians of the Eastern part of the Roman Empire. When Italy was overrun by the barbarians and when the Moslems conquered the Christians and took control of the Holy Land, Christians in the Middle East increasingly relied on the protection and leadership of the patriarch of Constantinople.

In 800, Pope Leo III proclaimed the Frankish King Charlemagne emperor of the Romans. Rome and Constantinople became separate centers of political power. The pope of Rome and the patriarch of Constantinople, each closely connected to his own political and cultural center, became religious rivals. Differences in culture and religious practices between Eastern and Western Christians increased a sense of separation in the Church. Attempts to ease tensions between popes and patriarchs suffered from the desire for domination by both leaders. Frequently there was a lack of mutual respect for legitimate differences in practice and worship between Eastern and Western Christianity.

The final split between the Eastern and Western Churches came in 1054, when Pope Leo IX and Patriarch Michael of Constantinople disagreed over theological and political matters. In anger, representatives of the two major leaders of Christianity condemned one another and effectively brought about the first major division in the Body of Christ. Attempts at reconciliation bore no fruit and the split between the Eastern Orthodox and Catholic Churches has yet to be healed fully.

The Eastern Christian Churches which do not enjoy full union with the pope are referred to as "Eastern Orthodox." There are other Eastern Christian Churches, however, that have reestablished full union with the bishop of Rome and the Catholic Church. In so doing these Eastern Catholic Churches (also called "Eastern Catholic Rites") have retained their special liturgical languages and traditions. The traditions they follow are some of the most ancient in the Church: the Coptic (Egyptian), the Ethiopic, Syrian, Malankarese, and Malabarese (South Indian), Maronite (Lebanese), Greek, Melkite (Byzantine), Russian, Ruthenian (Ukranian), Chaldean (Syrian-Persian), and Armenian Rites.

Eastern Catholic Churches in union with the pope observe slightly different rules and procedures from those followed by Western or Roman Rite Catholics. For example, Eastern Catholic Rites allow married men to become priests. Eastern Rite Catholics also have their own system of bishops and dioceses.

The Protestant Reformation — 1521

Although the Christian Church was split along Eastern and Western traditions with little hope for reconciliation, both East and West maintained authentic beliefs, sacraments, and authority structures. At the start of the sixteenth century, however, many issues and problems within the Western Church contributed to further divisions.

At about the same time that Columbus was discovering America, European Christianity was beset with numerous problems. Several recent popes had been more politically than spiritually inclined and some bishops lived in a style more suited to princes than spiritual shepherds. Many priests and deacons were poorly educated and thus limited in their ability to offer sound pastoral ministry. Many Catholics were superstitious and subscribed to an almost magical view of the sacraments. Many others believed that salvation could be earned by buying indulgences.

In the face of these problems and abuses, some monks, theologians, bishops, and preachers attempted to reform the Church. One reformer managed to gain the attention of the whole Church. He was the German Augustinian monk, Martin Luther.

Luther lived and taught at the University of Wittenberg in Germany. He sought enlightenment by studying Sacred Scripture and focused on the Letter to the Romans where he read that "the one who is righteous by faith shall live" (Romans 1:17). This Scripture passage changed Luther's life. For the first time Luther felt freed from his repeated attempts to work his way into heaven. He began to teach that faith in Jesus Christ was sufficient for salvation. He desired to reform the Catholic Church's teachings on the sacraments and the sacrificial nature of the Mass. He also called for greater use of the Bible by the faithful and suggested that the Mass be celebrated in the language of the people rather than in Latin. He called for a reform of Church hierarchy and the priesthood that would give the baptized faithful a larger role in spreading Christ's message of salvation. He also demanded an end to the abuses connected with the sale of indulgences.

As Luther's calls for reform were not adequately considered by Rome, he became increasingly convinced of his own opinions. Eventually Luther was labeled a heretic and excommunicated from the Catholic Church. He then left the Augustinian monastery, married, and started his own school of theology.

The princes of northern Germany took advantage of Luther's actions to set up their own Christian communities in an attempt to gain independence from the pope. Many princes adhered to the principle that all their subjects should worship in the same Christian community. For this reason large groups of Christians were ordered not to follow the directives of the pope but to worship in these new Christian communities. The princes protested any toleration of Catholics in their realms and thus earned the name "Protestant."

Meanwhile in Switzerland, Ulrich Zwingli and the *Anabaptists* began their reform by taking Luther's teachings a step further. Zwingli and other Anabaptists denied the existence of original sin in the individual person and completely rejected the baptism of infants. They also disagreed with Luther concerning the Real Presence of Christ in the Eucharist. Luther had rejected the Catholic explanation for the Real Presence, but still believed that Christ was present in the bread and wine. Zwingli and his followers denied the Real Presence altogether.

The French theologian John Calvin, living in Switzerland, further developed the Protestant Reform by setting up a strict Christian government in Geneva. Calvin taught that infants born of Christian parents were saved on account of the parents' faith and therefore could be baptized. He shunned church adornment and ceremony, priestly vestments, and organ music. He emphasized education, sound Bible teaching, and lively preaching as the way to holiness. His teachings emphasized the total depravity of the human person. He taught that Christ died only for the elect who were predestined to heaven because they could not resist God's saving grace once it was offered. Like the other Protestants, Calvin rejected the idea of a celibate priesthood and emphasized the priesthood of the laity.

By the middle of the sixteenth century the reforms fostered by Luther and Calvin had spread throughout Northern Germany, Holland, Switzerland, Scandinavia, and parts of France.

In England the Reformation took hold more gradually than in other parts of Europe. King Henry VIII split with the Catholic

Church when the pope refused to grant an annulment for his first marriage when his wife could not produce a male heir. During Henry's reign, the Church in England remained essentially Catholic in its beliefs and practices, although Henry confiscated much church property and set himself up as the head of the Church of England.

Henry's son, Edward VI, under the influence of the archbishop of Canterbury Thomas Cramner, completed the break with Rome by changing the language of the Mass to English, eliminating the requirement of priestly celibacy, and deemphasizing all the sacraments except Baptism and Eucharist. Many Catholic traditions and devotions remained in the Church of England, including a hierarchical structure of government and the monastic tradition. The *Thirty-nine Articles of Faith* and *Book of Common Prayer* became the normative guide to doctrine, worship, and private spirituality.

Except for a brief period of return to the Roman Catholic fold under Henry's elder daughter, the Catholic Queen Mary, England remained staunchly independent of Rome. Queen Elizabeth I, Mary's successor, tolerated no religious extremism and set a middle course between Protestantism and Catholicism for the English Christian Church, which is often referred to as the Anglican or Episcopal Church.

The Catholic Church responded to the Protestant Reformation by calling an ecumenical council which met in the northern Italian city of Trent from 1545-1563. During the Council of Trent the Catholic Church clarified many of its teachings and enacted new procedures to combat the prevalent abuses of power and authority. The council addressed the theological issues raised by the Protestants, changed the way in which bishops would shepherd their flocks, established seminaries for the training of priests, and renewed the liturgy of the Mass and the other sacraments.

The Church also found new missionary vigor as a result of the Council of Trent. Priests were sent to Africa, India, the Far East, and the New World, where they preached the gospel and established Catholic missions. Also, many Protestants in Europe were brought back to the Catholic fold.

From the end of the Council of Trent until the late nineteenth century, the Catholic Church enjoyed a prolonged period of relative calm. The twentieth century, however, has brought many new issues to the attention of the Catholic Church and its leaders. One of these issues is the reunification of all Christians. Just as the divisions of Christianity took place over a period of hundreds of years, so the process of reunification will probably not be quick. Education and information, prayer and good will, cooperation and communication will all serve to bring new unity to the Body of Christ. The remaining chapters of this book provide basic information and practical suggestions for ecumenical growth and Christian unity.

2.
Similarities and Differences Among Christians

A. Similarities

While history, culture, and personalities can bring about differences that seem insurmountable, Catholic, Orthodox, Anglican, and Protestant Christians actually do share many common beliefs and practices. This can give rise to a sense of hopefulness but should not lead to a false sense of optimism about the reunion of divided Christendom. This chapter summarizes some of the basic similarities and differences among Christian Churches on key elements of the faith.

1. Jesus Christ and the Trinity

Most Christians find their faith best expressed in the truths contained in the Apostles' and Nicene Creeds. All Christians believe in Jesus Christ as Savior and Lord, the one sent by God who died for the sins of the world and rose from the dead to the glory of heaven. Christians from the Catholic, Orthodox, Anglican, and most Protestant traditions accept Christ as the second person of the Blessed Trinity. They view him as being truly God and truly human.

2. Sacred Scripture

After Jesus Christ, the Bible is the second most important element uniting Christians. Christians believe that the Bible is a supreme source of truth, doctrine, comfort, and inspiration for all people.

The number and content of the books of the Bible are not agreed upon by all Christians. Also the interpretation and relative importance given to certain books and passages of the Bible vary from group to group. These issues are a source for fruitful dialogue, since many apparent disagreements in biblical interpretation are often more a case of differing emphasis than of doctrinal disunity.

3. Prayer

God is not just totally "other"; God is also intimately involved in the lives of all people. Christians are able to communicate with God through prayer and the power of the Holy Spirit. Christ, the mediator between God and all people, brings all prayers to the throne of the Father. In prayer God both hears the needs of people and communicates love, forgiveness, and healing. For the faithful Christian, prayer is the constant link to the heavenly Father, who cares for his children according to their specific needs. Praying together can be one of the primary ways to bring Christians together, no matter what their denomination or tradition.

4. Baptism

While many of the Christian Churches do not recognize all seven sacraments as the Catholic and Orthodox Churches do,

Baptism is the universal Christian sacrament. It is recognized as the entrance into the Christian family: "Baptism constitutes the sacramental bond of unity existing among all who through it are reborn. But Baptism, of itself, is only a beginning, a point of departure, for it is wholly directed toward the acquiring of fullness of life in Christ. Baptism is thus ordained toward a complete profession of faith, a complete incorporation into the system of salvation, such as Christ himself willed it to be, and finally, toward a complete integration into Eucharistic communion" (*Decree on Ecumenism,* #22).

Acceptance of the validity of Baptism performed in all Christian communities is at the forefront of ecumenical relations. There remains, however, some disagreement among Christians concerning adult versus infant baptism and baptism by total immersion versus baptism by sprinkling or pouring of water. Many fundamentalist and all Baptist Christians insist upon adult-only baptism after a confession of faith is pronounced. Christians of the Orthodox, Catholic, Anglican, and many Protestant traditions believe that God is the source of faith for all people and that God transmits this through the believing community, thus enabling infants to be baptized.

5. Marriage

Most Christians view marriage as a sacred commitment between the husband and wife that is blessed by God. Catholics and Orthodox Christians consider marriage as one of the sacraments. While Catholics maintain that the marriage vows can never be broken, most other Christians believe the permanence of the marriage vows is an ideal often not achieved. Thus, they are more understanding of divorce and remarriage within the Church.

6. Social and Personal Ethics

More and more Christians of all Churches and denominations are working together to promote issues of social justice. Protestants, Anglicans, Orthodox, and Catholics often collaborate both on the local and the global level to promote health care and housing for the poor, fair wages, honest government, the just settlement of labor disputes, the alleviation of hunger, arms control, and world peace.

In matters of individual morality, especially in the area of sexuality, Christians do not always agree. They often differ on the issue of birth control and the morality of abortion, although more and more Christian groups are adopting the belief that abortion is an evil to be condemned.

B. Differences

If all Christians agreed on all matters of belief, morality, authority, and worship, there would be little need for ecumenical discussions and programs to promote Christian unity. The fact remains, however, that there are clear and recognizable differences between Christian Churches. It is these differences that must be acknowledged and that form the agenda for ecumenical activity.

1. Teaching Authority of the Church

Catholics believe that Christ gave his authority to teach to the twelve apostles. They, in turn, passed it on through the sacrament of Holy Orders to their successors, the pope and the bishops. Catholics believe that Saint Peter and his successors, the bishops of Rome, possess the authority from Christ to teach in his name.

Other Christian groups do not view the pope as the ultimate authority in the Christian world. While some Christian groups do have a system of bishops and dioceses, many other Christians consider the local pastor or a board of elders and deacons to be the chief authority.

2. *Scripture and Tradition*

In general, most Protestants rely heavily on the Bible as the authoritative expression of the will of God. They place less emphasis on Sacred Tradition and the teachings of Church leaders than do Catholic Christians.

3. *Justification and Salvation*

Catholics and other Christians are discussing this matter in order to learn and understand the varied and rich teachings on this matter. Basically, all talk of justification and salvation is an attempt to put into human words a divine concept. It tries to answer the question, "How are we made worthy of heaven?" For centuries Luther's "faith alone" was contrasted to the Catholic teaching of "faith and good works" as it was expressed in the Letter of James 2:14-26.

Neither Catholics nor other Christians can successfully reduce this teaching to a few words. Ecumenical discussions have shown that while there are differences in approach and terminology, general agreement is possible among Christians on the meaning of justification and salvation.

4. *The Validity of the Seven Sacraments*

Catholics believe in the authenticity of the seven sacraments. They link each of the sacraments to the actions and teachings of

Jesus. The Orthodox also accept the seven sacraments as coming from Christ. Many Anglican as well as Protestant congregations, however, consider Baptism and the Eucharist to be the only two sacraments. While these Christian groups celebrate marriage and confirmation, have ordination ceremonies, visit the sick, and see the need for repentance and conversion, they do not label these actions as sacraments.

Ecumenical discussion on these matters involves questions about the nature of the sacraments and the necessity of validly ordained ministers to celebrate the sacraments. Most Protestants believe that the valid celebration of the sacraments depends primarily on the faith of the believing community and not on the validity of the minister's ordination.

5. The Veneration of the Saints and the Virgin Mary

Catholics, Orthodox, and many Anglicans venerate the saints as heroic Christians and role models. Saints, though they reside in glory, are still members of the Church, mystically united to the Church on earth through the Holy Spirit. For this reason Catholics, Orthodox, and Anglicans ask saints to intercede for them through the power of God's grace.

Most Protestants believe saints ought to be venerated as examples of virtue. They do not, however, find a scriptural basis to substantiate the belief that there can be prayerful communication between members of the Church on earth and the saved in heaven.

The Catholic Church teaches that Mary, the Mother of Jesus, is likewise to be revered as the Mother of God and the Mother of all Christians. The Catholic Church also teaches that she was sinless, that she remained a virgin, and that she was assumed into heaven, body and soul, at the end of her life. Christians of the Orthodox and Anglican traditions practice a similar devotion to Mary and celebrate many of her feasts during the liturgical year.

Most Protestants do not accord this level of attention to Mary. They honor her as Christ's Mother, as his first disciple, and as a holy woman. But they do not share the other beliefs that are part of the Catholic, Orthodox, and Anglican traditions.

3.
Understanding the Many Christian Communities

Christian Churches draw their principal focus from Christ. It is the teachings and actions of Jesus joined with his saving death and Resurrection that form the heart of all Christian religions. For Lutherans and Baptists as much as for Catholics, Jesus is the center of their life. At the same time, it is clear that all Christian Churches do not agree in their teachings about Jesus, God, the Bible, authority, morality, prayer, and spirituality. This chapter will briefly present some of the key beliefs of those Christian Churches, communities, and sects that are not in complete union with the Catholic Church.

A. The Eastern Orthodox

There are seven Orthodox Christian Churches which separated from the Roman Church in 1054 and which do not acknowledge the primacy of the bishop of Rome, the pope. They form a group of self-governing Churches with sixty million members worldwide. The patriarchs of Constantinople, Alexandria, Antioch, and Jerusalem have the first places of honor, owing to the ancient tradition that the apostles were associated with these four cities. Four other patriarchates have been formed in the course of history: the Bulgarian, Serbian, Russian, and Rumanian.

The patriarch of Constantinople is called the ecumenical patriarch, since he enjoys a position of special honor among Orthodox Christians. Although he does not exercise direct jurisdiction over all Orthodox Christians in the way that the pope does for all Catholic Christians, he is regarded highly by Catholics because of his place at the head of one of the oldest Christian communities.

The Orthodox regard Scripture as a source of revelation, but there is not total agreement with Catholics on the number and content of inspired books, particularly in the Old Testament. The seven sacraments are the same as in the Catholic Church, although Baptism, Confirmation, and Eucharist are all administered to infants. The eucharistic liturgies celebrated by the Orthodox are rich in tradition and ceremony, emphasizing the mystical union between the Church on earth and the heavenly hosts.

Orthodox may divorce and remarry validly several times. Married laymen may be ordained deacons and priests, but widowed priests may not remarry. Orthodox bishops must be celibates; they may be either monks or widowers.

Although separated from the Catholic Church for about nine hundred years, there are few doctrinal differences to overcome before reunion could occur. Most barriers to reunion are cultural and historical in nature. Both the pope of Rome and the patriarch of Constantinople have been working for reunion since 1964 when Pope Paul VI and Patriarch Athenagoras I met in Jerusalem. A 1987 meeting between Pope John Paul II and Patriarch Dimitrios I resulted in a joint declaration of ecumenical commitment expressing hope for the day "when the Eucharist will be celebrated in renewed faith, and in which full communion will be reestablished with a concelebration of the Eucharist."

In North America, the many divisions of the Orthodox Church can seem confusing to Christians. These divisions result from various ethnic identities, liturgical practices, usages of languages and calendars (Julian or Gregorian), and the many jurisdictional lines. It is especially difficult to distinguish between an Eastern *Catholic* Church and an Eastern *Orthodox* Church. Eastern Catholic Churches (also called "Uniate" Churches) generally use the name *Catholic* after their rite (for example, Greek Catholic Church or Melkite Catholic Church). The Orthodox Churches generally will have the name *Orthodox* or *Apostolic* in their titles, such as Armenian Apostolic Church or Greek Orthodox Church.

All Catholics may fulfill their Sunday obligation by attending Mass at an Eastern Catholic Church. Likewise, all Catholics can receive Communion at Eastern *Catholic* Churches. This cannot be done, however, in Eastern *Orthodox* Churches.

B. The Anglicans and Episcopalians

While the Roman Catholic Church views Orthodox more kindly than it views the Protestants and Anglicans, tremendous progress has been made in improving relations with Protestant and Anglican Christians since the Second Vatican Council.

Episcopalians are part of the worldwide Anglican communion who give primacy of honor to the Archbishop of Canterbury. Episcopalians are so called because they elect bishops (*Episcopoi* in Greek) to govern them. Episcopalians and Anglicans throughout the world often view themselves as observing a form of Christianity that stands midway between Roman Catholicism and Protestantism.

Much diversity is found in liturgical practice among Anglicans and Episcopalians around the world. Many emphasize traditional Catholic beliefs and practices. These groups, sometimes referred to as Anglo-Catholics or High Anglicans, foster a love for rich liturgical ceremonies, all seven sacraments, veneration of the saints, and frequent confession and communion.

In recent years the question of the ordination of women has become both a divisive issue in the Anglican communion and in ecumenical discussions between Anglicans and Catholics.

There are over forty-six million Anglicans worldwide, with almost three million in the United States and five hundred thousand in Canada.

C. The Mainline Protestants

Protestants profess most of the same beliefs that Catholics profess in the Apostles' and Nicene Creeds. At the same time, there can be great variation among Protestants — and between Protestants and Catholics — regarding the interpretation of the Bible, Church structure and authority, sacramental theology, morality, and personal piety.

There are approximately three-hundred twenty-five million Protestants in the world, seventy-five million of whom live in the United States with another eleven million living in Canada. This is compared to approximately eight-hundred million Catholics in the world, with fifty-two million in the United States and twelve million in Canada.

Because of the great diversity among Protestant denominations they are often separated into two groups: Mainline and Evangelical. Many large, older Protestant denominations, such as the Lutherans, Methodists, Congregationalists, and Presbyterians, have been put under the general heading of Mainline. These groups are generally more ecumenical and more open to contemporary interpretations of the Bible. Many have found renewed inspiration blending the teachings of the Reformers with certain liturgical and spiritual traditions from their Catholic roots and from contemporary Catholicism.

1. Lutherans

The seventy million Lutheran Christians throughout the world hold to the Augsburg Confession of 1530 which set out systematically the basic beliefs taught by Martin Luther. These beliefs included baptism for children, confession of sins, and the spiritual presence of Christ in the Eucharist. Lutherans in the United States and Canada range from the biblically conservative to the mildly liberal. Characteristic of nearly all Lutherans is a clearly documented series of beliefs supported by rigorous theological reasoning. Lutherans have been at the forefront among Protestants in the areas of education and liturgical reform.

2. Methodists

The Methodist community began with the eighteenth century attempt by John and Charles Wesley to reform the Anglican Church. The Wesleys emphasized personal conversion and holiness by following a simple "method" of piety. Their attempts at reform were rejected by the Anglican Church in England, but their success in the United States was phenomenal. Of the twenty million Methodists throughout the world, over half are in North America.

Methodists recognize four main sources and guidelines for Christian theology: Scripture, tradition, experience, and reason. Some Methodists use a modified Anglican book of common prayer for worship. Many celebrate infrequent and simple communion services. Some view smoking, alcohol, dancing, and gambling as obstacles to true holiness.

3. Congregationalists

Congregationalism describes the form of government practiced by the descendants of John Calvin. Each individual congregation is responsible for itself alone, using democratic principles to elect elders and deacons who direct the activities of the congregation. Congregationalists are a diverse group, although most belong to the United Church of Christ, which upholds many of the traditions of the Puritans who first came to New England. Many Congregationalists maintain a keen sensitivity to social issues and some tend to take liberal positions on moral issues.

4. Presbyterians

Presbyterians are the descendants of Scottish and English Puritans and are rooted in the Reformed Tradition of John Calvin. Like their Dutch Reformed cousins, many Presbyterians emphasize the absolute sovereignty of God and the spiritual helplessness of humanity. Some Presbyterians were on the front lines of controversy in the early twentieth century as they fought against Modernists who took a liberal view of the Bible. These Presbyterians helped to popularize the *fundamentals* of the faith which formed the foundation for twentieth-century fundamentalism and biblical literalism, as well as the growth of Evangelicalism.

Presbyterian refers to a form of church government brought to Scotland by John Knox. Elected elders oversee individual congregations, but the larger church exercises supervision over the congregations through presbyteries or associations of churches in a given area. There are almost four million Presbyterians in the United States and Canada.

D. The Evangelical and Fundamentalist Protestants

Evangelical Protestants are distinct from mainline Protestants in that they tend to be more conservative doctrinally and theologically. By definition, they emphasize the spreading of the Good News, the *Evangelium*. Most are characterized by strong preaching, intense missionary activity, extensive outreach programs, personal conversion or *born again* experiences, and a very conservative interpretation of the Bible as the sole source of doctrine and inspiration. Evangelicals base their faith on the *fundamentals* of Christianity: the atoning death and saving Resurrection of Christ, the inerrancy of the Bible, and the Second Coming of Christ. Evangelicals can be found as individuals within a mainline church or as a whole congregation which has an evangelical outlook.

Fundamentalist Protestants are distinguished from many Evangelicals by their literal interpretation of the Bible. They rely on it as a source of historical and scientific, as well as spiritual, truth. They sometimes are characterized by a lack of toleration toward others. Frequently they promote rigid role definitions for spouses and children and are preoccupied with the events surrounding the Second Coming of Christ and the end of the world. Fundamentalists form their own recognizable groups. They also may be found within many Evangelical communities. However, because of Fundamentalists' narrow world view and their separatist tendencies, many conservative Christians prefer to be called Evangelical.

1. Baptists

The approximately two dozen Baptist denominations, representing nearly twenty-six million people, constitute the largest Protestant group in North America. Originating with the Anabaptist Movement of 1525, today's Baptists call for baptism of adult believers by total immersion. Some Baptists believe *once saved, always saved,* which means that once an adult has given his or her life to Christ, he or she will endure to the end; salvation is assured and absolute. Even if believers fall into sin through neglect or temptation, they shall be kept safe by faith and the power of God unto salvation.

Baptists do not use the term *sacrament* to describe Baptism and Holy Communion. They refer to them as *ordinances* given by Christ, but not outward signs which impart grace.

2. Classical Pentecostals

Classical Pentecostals find some of their deepest roots in the preaching of John Wesley and the holiness tradition. Strongly advocating speaking in tongues, interpretation of tongues, physical healing, and other gifts of the Holy Spirit, the Pentecostal Movement has blossomed since it got a major start at the Azuza Street Mission in Los Angeles in 1906. Pentecostals insist on the need for baptism of the Spirit in addition to water baptism. Many also insist on the need to manifest the gift of tongues in order to prove that one has been baptized in the Spirit. There are nearly ten million Pentecostals worldwide and three million in America. They are the fastest growing group in missionary countries, especially in Latin America. Like other evangelicals, Pentecostals rely on the authority of the Bible alone, although for some, personal revelations through the power of the Holy Spirit carry much weight.

3. Charismatics

Charismatic Christians are those of traditional Protestant or Anglican backgrounds who have experienced the baptism of the Holy Spirit and who subscribe to the use of tongues and other spiritual gifts or *charisms*. The difference between charismatics and classical Pentecostals is that charismatics remain in their religious traditions, avoid the excesses of Pentecostalism, and do not insist that every person exhibit the gift of tongues. Prayer groups and Bible studies constitute their support network within the charismatic communities. (**Note:** There are also Catholic charismatics who integrate the Spirit-filled, Bible-centered charismatic Christianity with their Catholic beliefs and practices.)

E. The New Thought Movement

The New Thought movement covers a wide spectrum of groups which insist that people need not believe in sickness, evil, or poverty. Much New Thought theology is rooted in Gnosticism: It claims a need for a special knowledge not found in the normal channels of divine revelation. This special knowledge is supplied to the faithful through doctrinal teaching and writings other than the Bible.

New Thoughters do not draw a sharp line between God and the human person. They often verge on pantheism. They admire the moral teachings of Jesus but reject the dogmas of original sin, the Trinity, the atonement, and salvation. New Thought teaches that a person can always apply a spiritual solution to his or her problems; in this way he or she can achieve health, wealth, and happiness.

The Christian Scientists would be one example of a New Thought movement. Mary Baker Eddy of Boston began the

Christian Science Church in the late nineteenth century by combining spiritualism, faith healing, pantheism, and a highly optimistic view of humanity. Christian Scientists, like other New Thoughters, believe that physical illness is a symptom of wrong thinking. Such wrong thinking may be cured through the proper spiritual channels using trained *practitioners*. Strict observers shun the use of medicines and hospitals, tobacco, caffeine, and alcohol. Mrs. Eddy's book, *Science and Health With Key to the Scriptures,* is considered to be as inspired as the Bible.

F. Christian Sects

Certain groups indigenous to the United States and Canada have developed significant followings. These sects purport to be truly Christian in their teachings, although they are far removed from many basic elements of Christianity.

1. Jehovah Witnesses

Jehovah Witnesses got their start in 1872. Original adherents awaited the Second Coming of Christ in 1914. When Christ did not materialize, church leaders insisted that he did return, but secretly, to establish an invisible kingdom. He was supposed to come in 1925 to destroy the earth and save all Jehovah Witnesses. The date of Christ's return was revised to 1975 and then again to 2010.

The real authority behind the Jehovah Witnesses is the Brooklyn-based *Watchtower Bible and Tract Society.* This publishing house is the exclusive supplier of Witness material which all members are required to study and sell. Jehovah Witnesses do not consider themselves a formal religion since they believe all religions are works of the devil. Jesus is not God, but the reincarnation of the Archangel Michael. They do not believe in the Trinity, in hell, purgatory, or the immortality of the soul. They reject all traditional Christian beliefs which cannot be proven by the Bible alone. They believe that when Christ finally returns, 144,000 Jehovah Witnesses, a number found in the Book of Revelation, will be saved and go to live in the new heaven. All other worthy Jehovah Witnesses will live on a new earth. Everyone else will simply cease to exist.

2. Unitarian-Universalists

With less than 200,000 members, Unitarian-Universalists exert a disproportionate influence in politics and business. Unitarians find their roots in Arianism, an early Church heresy that taught that Jesus was a man but not fully God. They reject the dogma of the Trinity as a later addition to Christianity. Their hallmark is freedom of religion and belief. In 1961 the Unitarians merged with the Universalists, who formerly were Trinitarian but who themselves embraced Unitarianism in the nineteenth century.

Unitarian-Universalists have had their greatest influence in New England where they got their start. Many Congregationalist assemblies were split as some members began Unitarian congregations. Unitarians are known for upholding human rights, and were some of the first people on record against slavery. Today they advocate secular humanism and universal salvation. They permit their members to hold almost any beliefs and still remain in the congregation.

3. Church of Jesus Christ of Latter-Day Saints (Mormons)

Mormons believe that Christ preached to the American Indians after his Ascension and founded a church among them for the Western Hemisphere. The history of these events was supposedly revealed on golden tablets found in upstate New York in 1827 by Joseph Smith. Mormons believe that Smith reestablished the Church of Christ which had been wiped out in the Americas.

Mormons are *polytheists;* they believe there are many gods for many worlds. In fact, God is human, and each person lived with God in a previous existence. After death each person can become a god for his or her own planet, provided he or she has been baptized a Mormon.

Mormon government is hierarchical, with presidents, apostles, bishops, priests, and elders. They practice secret rituals in their temple, including proxy baptism and condemnation of Catholics and Protestants for having inadequate beliefs. Marriage is considered the norm for every Mormon and large families are encouraged. They believe that polygamy is the divine pattern of marriage, although most Mormons are very respectful of civil law and therefore do not practice polygamy. Mormon life is highly regulated from cradle to grave with strict personal moral standards.

4. Seventh-Day Adventists

Although Adventists appear to be nothing more than conservative Protestants who happen to celebrate the Sabbath on Saturday, there are many departures from traditional Protestantism in their beliefs. Their views of the human person and their beliefs about death and afterlife are unique. Adventists abstain from liquor and tobacco as a test of their faith. Those who lapse into such habits are excommunicated. They also observe Jewish dietary laws; for health reasons most are vegetarians. Adventists operate one of the largest parochial school systems in America as well as a vast health-care and missionary network. They do not object to serving in the armed forces but choose medical duty over bearing arms. While they believe that they alone constitute the true church, they recognize there are good Christians in other denominations and faiths.

G. Christian Cults

Christian cults are characterized by the veneration of a living leader — a powerful speaker and teacher who offers personal revelation from God. These cults have a veneer of Christianity in their ritual, terminology, personal morality, and use of the Bible, although one could question whether they are truly Christian groups. They frequently target young people who are looking for idealized and disciplined spiritual lives and close personal relationships. The mind control and high-energy activity used to keep followers submissive can lead to serious problems for the young followers, especially if they become disillusioned with the organization.

1. The Unification Church

This Asiatic cult is the creation of the Korean evangelist, Sun Myung Moon. He claims that at the age of sixteen he was visited by Jesus and given a new revelation. This and other revelations were compiled in the cult's basic text, *Divine Principle*. Moon believes the Bible was written in code and that he is God's chief interpreter.

Basic to Unification theology is the concept of the three Adams. The first Adam failed his mission and committed original sin with Eve. Jesus, the second Adam, failed his mission and was crucified. The Reverend Moon is assumed to be the third Adam and, according to his personal revelations, will succeed in his ministry.

The Unification Church has no ordained ministers or sacraments, but they do arrange marriages between their members. They are expected to give up alcohol, drugs, tobacco, and illicit sex. They are best known for raising millions of dollars by selling flowers, peanuts, and incense in airports and on street corners.

2. Church of Scientology

This group found its start in 1950 with the science-fiction writer L. Ron Hubbard and his best-selling book *Dianetics*. Dianetics is a process in which individuals find growth and peace by confessing the details of their past lives to an auditor (a minister of the Church of Scientology). Even though an introductory course in scientology costs only $15, a devotee can easily spend as much as $5,000 for the necessary auditing sessions which lead to a state of intellectual and spiritual renewal called the *clear* status. Scientology claims a membership in the millions, but a reasonable estimate of active membership in the United States is about thirty thousand.

3. "The Way"

The spiritual father of *The Way* is Victor Paul Vierwille, an ex-minister of the Evangelical and Reformed Church. He maintains that God has spoken to him audibly and revealed the true understanding of the Bible and of Christianity, lost since the early days of the Church. His followers are often college-age students who take his courses and are instructed in the Bible and in speaking in tongues. Vierwille's teaching is not traditionally Protestant, although his techniques resemble some of those used by campus groups such as Intervarsity Christian Fellowship and Campus Crusade for Christ.

(**Author's Note:** For further information see William J. Whalen's book *Separated Brethren,* Our Sunday Visitor Press, 1979. That book was most helpful in the composition of this chapter.)

4.
Understanding Non-Christian Religions

In addition to the *Decree on Ecumenism,* the Second Vatican Council issued a *Declaration on the Relation of the Church to Non-Christian Religions.* This document offers guidelines on how Catholics ought to view non-Christians (Jews, Moslems, Buddhists, etc.).

The document explains that the Catholic Church holds in highest regard the members of the Jewish faith, the sons and daughters of Abraham who are descendants of God's Chosen People, the Israelites. Since Jesus the Messiah was born of a Jewish mother and actively practiced the Hebrew faith, there is no doubt that the Christian faith finds its roots in Judaism. Catholics would do well to learn about Judaism since many Catholic liturgical traditions and theological understandings have their roots in the traditions of ancient Israel.

The Church repudiates any form of anti-Semitism and regrets incidents where Jews were persecuted by Christians and coerced to give up their faith to be baptized. Even though they have not recognized Jesus as the Messiah, Jews are not to be spoken of as rejected or accursed.

The Catholic Church also has a high regard for Moslems.

They, like the Jews, find their roots in Abraham, as descendants of his son Ishmael. These people worship the one true God, the Creator of heaven and earth. Moslems consider Jesus a great prophet and honor his virgin Mother Mary. They await the day of judgment and the reward of God following the resurrection of the dead.

Caution needs to be exercised when identifying Moslems. They have a genuine faith tradition and are not accurately represented by the fundamentalist Moslem sects such as those found in contemporary Iran, who advocate the violent overthrow of the Western World.

Buddhism testifies to the essential inadequacy of this changing world. It proposes a way of life by which people can, with confidence and trust, attain a state of perfect liberation and reach supreme illumination either through their own efforts or by the aid of divine help.

In Hinduism believers explore the divine mystery and express it both in the limitless riches of myth and the accurately defined insights of philosophy. They seek release from the trials of the present life by ascetical practices, profound meditation, and recourse to God in confidence and love.

The Catholic Church and most other Christian groups recognize elements of truth in all world religions. In today's world where religious harmony is a valued goal, each Church and religious group is asked to adopt a balanced position toward other religious groups. Holy wars and wholesale conversions to one particular religion or denomination are out of step with the principles of religious freedom enunciated by the Second Vatican Council in its *Declaration on Religious Freedom*.

The Catholic Church urges its members to enter into discussion and collaboration with members of other religions in a spirit of prudence and charity. In this way they can witness to their own faith and way of life, and acknowledge, preserve, and encourage the growth of spiritual and moral truths among other Christians and non-Christians.

It should be noted that contact between Catholics and non-Christians is most properly called "interfaith relations," not "ecumenical activities." Ecumenism refers to relations among Christian groups for whom it is possible to become united in Christ.

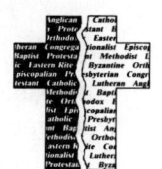

5.
Ecumenism — Healthy and Unhealthy

The *Decree on Ecumenism* strikes a conciliatory chord. While the decree clearly states that the true and indivisible Church of Christ is said to *subsist in* the Roman Catholic Church, it also acknowledges that Protestants belong to *communions* of faith in Christ which are, to one degree or another, united to the one true Church of Christ (see *Decree on Ecumenism,* #4). The Orthodox Churches are described as true Churches since they have maintained apostolic succession and celebrate true and authentic sacraments (see *Decree on Ecumenism,* #14-18).

Principles of Healthy Ecumenism

Within the *Decree on Ecumenism* and in ecumenical writings developed within the Catholic Church at the international, national, and local levels since the Council, one can discover certain elements of healthy ecumenism.

First, there should be an attitude of understanding and openness and a willingness to establish solid relationships with other Christians. If one Christian says to another, "My Church is the best and yours is all wrong," ecumenical growth will be impossible. There is no benefit in passing judgment on the willingness of any community to be faithful to the gospel. Participants in ecumenical exchanges must exhibit a genuine willingness to learn and grow — whether it be a husband and wife of different Christian Churches or two theologians from divergent Christian traditions.

Second, there must be a healthy respect for differences in history, tradition, and terminology. While an attitude of equality and openness among participants is important, all doctrinal or theological positions are not equal. Honest differences must be noted and accepted. When Christians of different communities gather for a wedding in a Catholic Church, it might seem like a good time to invite all the participants to receive Communion. When the members of different Churches do not agree on the meaning of the Eucharist, however, it is not proper to invite everyone to receive Communion. Often such situations of division become the source of further fruitful discussion and ecumenical growth.

Third, those who direct ecumenical activity ought to have the necessary competence in theology as well as the necessary pastoral skills. While much can be gained by the participants in ecumenical prayer services or interfaith Bible study groups, it is important that the leaders of such activities understand the traditions and teachings of the different Christian communities represented in the group. Knowledgeable ecumenical leaders will explain similarities and differences and help the participants understand the different traditions.

Fourth, Christians involved in ecumenical dialogue ought to know the basic teachings and practices of their Church without overstating or minimizing them. They should be familiar with the relationship between doctrines and should take into account legitimate theological diversity within the Church's teachings.

This involves reading and study as well as prayer and personal reflection.

Unhealthy Ecumenism Poses Problems

Not all ecumenical activity is automatically a success. Instead of growth and greater understanding in the faith, some Christians find ecumenical activities confusing and disconcerting. There are several situations to be avoided in ecumenical activities, services, and dialogues.

First, ecumenism is not primarily a time to make converts. While ecumenism affords a time for teaching others about one's faith, it is wrong for any one group to proselytize or force its faith upon others. Rather, by firm conviction and devout practice, each Christian can witness to his or her relationship with God and thereby help other Christians and non-Christians to draw closer to the Lord and to the truths of the Christian faith.

Second, unguided ecumenical activity can create misunderstanding. On official international levels ecumenical activity has flourished because it has been carefully monitored. On the local level, however, what sometimes has passed for ecumenism has damaged the cause of true ecumenism. When people engage unknowingly in unhealthy ecumenical activity, misunderstanding and mistrust can occur. When well-meaning but uninformed persons do not comprehend long-standing theological and doctrinal differences, they may become frustrated and give up on ecumenical efforts. In so doing they miss many opportunities to build bridges between Christians.

Third, ecumenism can cause confusion about one's own faith and practice. Since the Second Vatican Council, many Catholics have felt insecure about their faith and have been confused with external changes in liturgical practice. Ecumenically minded persons ought to be careful in dealing with those who may be uncomfortable with changes in their own Church and recognize that it is best to move slowly in ecumenical dialogue in order to prevent needless upset and to preserve correct doctrine and Church discipline.

Fourth, confusing terminology can add to an unhealthy ecumenical atmosphere. Catholics who hear about *born again* and *Spirit-filled* experiences do not always associate these terms with the more common expressions like *conversion of heart* and *being filled with God's grace*. Some Christians think that if a person does not use their language and terminology, then that person should not be considered a true Christian. It is vital that Christians learn the meaning of different theological terms in order to understand one another. It would help if people used biblical terminology and references whenever possible to help explain their beliefs and practices.

Regardless of these potential complications and difficulties, ecumenism is ultimately worthwhile. The positive results can outweigh the difficulties. It is worth the effort to reunite the Body of Christ.

6. Ecumenism in Marriage and the Home

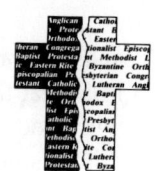

One of the most positive influences of ecumenical growth has been on families where each parent is of a different religious tradition. So-called "interfaith marriages" have often proven to be special gifts to the Church as well as to family life. Interfaith marriages have led to extended families which sometimes come from several faith traditions. This grassroots ecumenism is often the best kind as it brings people to a deeper understanding of many Christian traditions. It also helps them to experience firsthand the faith and goodness of members of other Christian Churches. At the same time, being sensitive to varying religious needs in the immediate family can present special challenges.

The Spiritual Unity of Marriage

When a man and woman plan to marry, their highest priority ought to be whether or not they are compatible. If the two people have very different value systems, if their personalities do not mesh, if they cannot tolerate each other's foibles and habits, then little hope can be given for a successful marriage.

Spiritual compatibility is also an important factor for a successful marriage. Since Christian marriage is a sacrament and a union of mind, body, and spirit with God and the Church, it is vital that the couple know about each other's relationship with God and how God becomes present in their lives. It is for this reason, among others, that the Catholic Church teaches that a Catholic ought to marry another Catholic. A common faith experience can form a solid foundation on which to build true spiritual unity in marriage.

Interchurch and Interfaith Marriages

The Church recognizes that in pluralistic societies Catholic men and women do not always fall in love with other Catholics. This is why the Church allows Catholics validly to marry Christians who are not Catholics (interchurch marriages) and even to marry people who are not Christians (interfaith marriages). In the marriage preparation for such couples, some time ought to be spent talking about spiritual compatibility and clarifying the issues involved in an interfaith and interchurch marriage.

Each partner needs to learn about the partner's faith and religious experience. Every effort should be made to emphasize common elements of faith and to understand differences. Each partner may need some instruction as to the workings of the other's Church or faith and should be invited to explore its beliefs and practices in greater depth, either before or after the wedding. It seems best if neither party pressures the other to join his or her faith community, either before or after the wedding.

Sharing Traditions With Children

If possible, both spouses in an interfaith or interchurch marriage ought to practice their own faith with regularity, both to maintain a healthy relationship with God and his or her faith community, and as a good example for the children. As the children grow, it will be important for both spouses to share what they have in common. The Scriptures, the events of Christ's life, the liturgical seasons, and the religious traditions surrounding the holidays are important focal points for all Christians. Christians and non-Christians can also find common beliefs and religious practices.

The Catholic Church instructs its members in interchurch and interfaith marriages that they should do all that they can to see that the children will be baptized and raised as Catholics. It is also important, however, that the children have a chance to learn about both faith traditions. Especially when the Catholic partner practices his or her faith with less regularity than the other partner, it is important that the children be exposed to the faith tradition of the parent who practices the faith more actively.

When Children Change Churches or Religions

There is perhaps no greater heartbreak for Christian parents than when one of their children changes his or her faith commitment. How do parents and family members deal sensitively with this issue?

First, it is important to protect young people from the wrong religious influence. Parents ought to find out about any youth program or organization which their children wish to attend. The best way to deal with religious youth groups which attract children is to work with their leadership and seek ways to form a truly ecumenical atmosphere for youth.

Second, parents have to maintain an open line of communication with their older children. When children are away at college, pressured with schoolwork, and sometimes lonely, some religious groups and cults sweep the campus for prospective members. How do parents find out if their child is being unduly influenced by a cult group? The best way is to listen carefully to their children when they come home for vacation. If they seem preoccupied with faith issues, they need to feel comfortable discussing these concerns with their parents.

Third, parents need to be patient. Frequently young adults go through a time of asserting their independence. They feel a need to doubt and question what they have been taught about their faith. During this time they can benefit from their parents' prayer, the steadfast witness of their parents' faith, and a freedom to question and grow. From such questioning comes the growth that moves a faith from a childhood to adult level.

In the end, when one's child leaves the Church to join another religious group, parents and other family members need to show the kind of love and acceptance Christ would show, without feeling it necessary to approve of the religion itself. God sometimes leads people down many roads before they find their final spiritual home.

7.
Ecumenism Among Family and Relatives

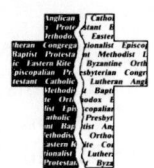

It is important for Catholics to be sensitive and aware when relatives or in-laws are members of other Christian Churches or of non-Christian religions. The members of other Christian groups and other religions are often quite willing to talk about their faith and the traditions of their religion. This can be a good educational opportunity and can lead to further discussion about the Catholic faith as well.

Sensitivity ought to be shown with regard to special needs or traditions held by members of other Churches and religions. Kosher food for Jewish relatives, respect for the Friday night to Saturday night Sabbath for both Jews and Adventist Christians, use of alcoholic beverages, and choosing appropriate forms of entertainment and music for some Evangelical Christians are some practical issues which may need to be addressed.

When Relatives Join Other Churches and Religions

Sometimes relatives leave the Catholic Church to join another religion or another Christian community. Frequently Jews and Moslems insist that their children marry someone of the same faith. Pressure to convert is often brought to bear upon non-Jews and non-Moslems when they enter into marriage with Jews and Moslems. Sometimes Catholics find their spouse's Church or religion more attractive and eventually decide to join officially. Faithful Catholics sometimes view these changes as "giving up the true faith." Family arguments and heartache can result if such conversions are not handled in a Christian way.

It is hoped that, if asked, any advice will urge the potential convert seriously to reconsider his or her plans to leave the Catholic Church or to leave behind his or her faith in Christ. It is appropriate to point out the important truths which the Catholic may be giving up and to urge him or her to seek the advice of a knowledgeable priest, deacon, or religious educator. In the end, if a Catholic leaves the Church, their Catholic friends and relatives must assume it was done in good faith and refrain from judgment. They ought to maintain a close and friendly relationship with the former Catholic if at all possible.

The Catholic Church recently has changed one important discipline which affects the marital status of Catholics who have joined another Church. It is now the case that if a Catholic officially and publicly joins a Protestant community, he or she is viewed by the Catholic Church as a Protestant. If he or she then decides to marry a Protestant in a Protestant ceremony, the Catholic Church will consider it a valid marriage.

When Relatives Join the Catholic Church

On occasion a relative may inquire about joining the Catholic faith, perhaps because of the witness of someone in the family. Such a relative ought to be fully supported by his or her Catholic family members and encouraged to take the necessary steps, provided that the person has considered all the implications of the decision, especially as it might impact upon the person's family of origin who may not be Catholic.

In this situation the Catholic Church has provided a special *Rite of Christian Initiation for Adults (RCIA)*. This rite is primarily for adults who have never been baptized but can be adapted for adults who have been baptized in one Christian communion and who ask to be received into full communion with the Catholic Church.

The RCIA provides an open-ended period of *inquiry* during which the candidate can explore the faith, deepen his or her relationship with God, and ask questions. Next follows a period of instruction called the *catechumenate,* based on the mysteries of the Catholic faith and the Scriptures used on Sundays. Eventually, the candidate receives the sacraments necessary for full *initiation:* Baptism (for those never before baptized), Confirmation, and Holy Eucharist. Finally there follows an additional period of instruction called the *Mystagogia*.

During the period in which the adult is involved in the RCIA, he or she will need help and support from the family and the parish. Built into the RCIA is the opportunity for the entire parish community to involve itself in the preparation and spiritual renewal of the candidates. In a special way, this can be an ecumenical activity of one's family and relatives.

8. Ecumenism in the Parish

The parish is not only where Catholics celebrate Mass and the sacraments, it is the best locale for getting to know neighbors and coming to deeper mutual understanding and appreciation for differing faith traditions. A parish either can foster or discourage healthy ecumenism. It can view relations with other Christians and members of other religions as an extra burden or as an opportunity for grace and growth.

Ecumenical relations ought to be entered into slowly, deliberately, and without naïveté. Time must be spent developing trust and personal relationships in any ecumenical group. Short-term or sporadically scheduled meetings are not sufficient to foster the kind of trust necessary to build bridges and break down barriers between separated Churches. Larger issues often must wait until each person involved feels comfortable enough to be open, honest, nondefensive, and loving with the other members of the group.

In both ecumenical and interfaith endeavors, every effort ought to be made to observe the principles of reciprocity and collaboration. As a general rule one should neither extend nor accept an invitation to participate in an ecumenical or interfaith activity unless one may extend or accept a similar invitation in return. Collaboration means that in planning any ecumenical or interfaith activity or service, there should be consultation among representatives of all the participating faiths or communions from the beginning.

There are many practical ways that a parish can initiate and nourish ecumenical and interfaith relations.

Prayer

All ecumenical and interfaith activity ought to be supported by personal prayer. If God is not behind all efforts, then ultimately they produce no fruit. It is good to begin all ecumenical activities with a brief period of prayer and Scripture reading to set the tone. The leader of prayer ought to pray as he or she is comfortable, according to his or her tradition. Public prayer ought to be as inclusive as possible without violating one's theology and beliefs. At the same time, Christians ought not hesitate to mention the name of Jesus Christ, even though non-Christians might be present.

It is important, however, not to make prayer a cause of contention and argument. For example, Catholics should be sensitive about using exclusively Catholic prayer forms such as the Hail Mary. Likewise, celebrations of the Eucharist are not appropriate, since they tend to highlight division and not commonality.

Public ecumenical prayer might take the form of prayer services for Thanksgiving, Palm Sunday, Good Friday, or Easter. Such services, if they are already a tradition in the community, might be good opportunities for communal public prayer, but they need not be the only opportunities.

Bible Study

Ecumenical Bible study groups can promote understanding and extend spiritual support to many, provided they do not deal with controversial or divisive subjects. The danger in any kind of

Bible study is literalism and fundamentalism. Catholics need to be wary of both. Study aids should not contradict a Catholic understanding of Scripture. Women's Aglow groups and Fellowship Bible Coffee groups are national organizations which foster ecumenical Bible study. There are many other study programs using video and audio cassettes which may be available in Christian bookstores or at diocesan offices of religious education.

Bible study among clergy based on the common lectionary readings for Sunday services can be a helpful way both of developing personal relationships among clergy and of preparing the sermon for the next week. Catholic, Lutheran, Episcopalian, and United Church of Christ lectionaries generally follow the same cycle of Bible readings.

Dialogue

Ecumenical and interfaith dialogue can take several forms. Members of a dialogue group may be clergy, laity, or both. Subjects can range from theological and doctrinal issues to spirituality and prayer, social and political issues, or particular community issues which need immediate attention. The group should not intend to resolve specific theological questions but should rather attempt to facilitate ongoing discussion and to increase understanding of different faiths. Such discussions can also lead to greater cooperation and a more broad-based relationship between two or more local faith communities. The boundaries for discussion as well as the format for the meetings ought to be worked out ahead of time.

Sharing of Pulpits

Sometimes the exchange of pulpits can be an opportunity for one pastor to get to know the congregation of another. The week of Christian Unity in January provides an annual opportunity for this practice. Obvious care must be taken that theology and doctrine be correct and that there is a previous understanding between the clergy concerning the subject on which to preach.

Church Covenanting

Some Catholic parishes have found it helpful to enter into covenants with particular local Christian congregations with whom they have a great deal in common. Covenanting is a way of bonding Christians of different faiths and yet maintaining individual identities. These special relationships among clergy and congregation can build lasting friendships and lead to much mutual growth, while addressing the issues which yet divide.

Church covenanting is not suitable for every parish, but it has been a fruitful experience for some throughout the country. There are cases where one worship center is used for more than one church congregation or even for a Christian parish and a Jewish synagogue. Schedules are worked out so that each group can worship separately, with full use of the physical plant. Such cooperation makes it much easier financially to satisfy the spiritual needs of a community and builds special relationships among people of faith.

Social Gatherings

Sometimes simple social gatherings with no particular spiritual motive can get ecumenical and interfaith relations started in a friendly manner. Almost anything that brings people together can be a reason to invite local Protestant, Anglican, or Orthodox congregations to a Catholic event. There are also occasions when it would be appropriate to invite members of other faiths. Sensitivity ought to be shown when refreshments or meals are served with regard to alcoholic beverages, fasting, abstinence, and other dietary laws.

Hospital and Prison Ministry

So much good can be done for the sick and for prisoners when Christians work together. For example, *Por Christo* is a non-profit group made up of volunteer medical professionals dedicated to working together with their South American counterparts to improve health standards in Latin America. *Por Christo* is a model which might be used to help the poor of America's urban and rural areas.

The style and goals of any ecumenical ministry ought to be discussed carefully. A ministerial strategy needs to be worked out and strictly adhered to, lest ecumenical efforts become counter-productive.

Military Chaplaincy

A great ecumenical success story can be found on many military and naval bases throughout the United States. By necessity, military chaplains of every faith find cooperation and mutual understanding to be beneficial not only to their individual ministries, but to the population they serve. Military service personnel and their families need special care due to the unusual nature of their working and living situations. Chaplains have found that interfaith communication is the best way to meet the needs of their faith communities. Perhaps chaplains could share their ecumenical success stories with other interested clergy groups who seek better relations.

9. Ecumenism in the Community

Sometimes being ecumenical has very little directly to do with religious services, theological discussion, or spiritual inquiry. In religiously mixed communities, large and small, it is vital that members of individual faith communities work together to address social and moral issues facing the community.

Many of these social and moral concerns have been addressed by theologians and Church leaders in a theoretical manner. Local religious groups, however, may find it necessary to address these issues in a more practical way as they touch their own communities. Rather than each parish church or religious group working independently, it is more effective if many groups work together to remedy social ills and change public policy. There are many issues where ecumenical concern and activity is quite appropriate.

Education

In the area of public education, people of all faiths ought to be very concerned not only with curriculum, but with some current philosophies of education. For example, even though "values clarification" at first appears to be an excellent way of teaching moral standards, it can end up relativizing morality and promoting an individualistic ethic which goes against the moral absolutes embodied in the Ten Commandments. Religious values become merely private values and can easily be dismissed as being narrow, sectarian, and a threat to the separation between Church and State.

Monitoring the content of sex-education programs is another area where people of many faiths can work together. Still another issue of concern is school-based health clinics. With their focus on the problem of teen pregnancies, the clinics may provide birth control information to the student without the parents' knowledge or consent. These clinics can undermine parental authority and Judeo-Christian morality.

Public Housing

Another area of concern is the issue of the homeless and the lack of affordable public housing. Increasingly, families and young adults are finding the street the only place to call home. Many emotionally disturbed adults, deinstitutionalized and frequently neglected, live disordered existences in many American cities. Religious leaders ought to better mobilize their congregations to lobby for affordable public housing which will be properly maintained by the local government and provide for those who have no other choice. They can also consider staffing and supporting shelters for the homeless.

Racial and Ethnic Tensions

Religious groups of every racial and ethnic background have succeeded in breaking down many racial barriers. However, the vision of Dr. Martin Luther King, a Baptist minister, is yet to be fully realized. The ecumenical cooperation which helped to bring equality to Black Americans can and must continue to work until bigotry against all racial and ethnic groups is wiped out.

As new groups of people emigrate to seek new opportunities in America, it is vital to incorporate them into the life of the community and to help them find stability by providing a worshiping community.

Labor Practices

The Catholic Church has been at the forefront in teaching about the rights and responsibilities of management and labor within society. From the social encyclicals of Pope Leo XIII in the late nineteenth century to the teachings of Pope John Paul II, the Church has upheld the dignity of the worker as part of God's plan for an ordered society. Catholics need to unite with members of other faiths to seek appropriate and decently paying jobs for all who would like to work.

Health Care

As health care costs balloon, increasingly large numbers of individuals cannot afford to get sick. Some of the largest health care systems in the United States, apart from those conducted by the federal government, are run by religious groups. It is ecumenically as well as socially vital that local congregations make themselves aware of community health needs and that they cooperate with other religious groups in order to influence the planning and establishment of health facilities and clinics in their communities.

Caring for the Elderly

As people live longer lives, the need for adequate nursing and convalescent homes will increase. Now is the time for ecumenical leadership to find ways to ease the burden of some senior citizens. It is also time to encourage senior citizens to become more involved in community and parish life. Today many elderly are healthy and financially independent. They may have a great deal of free time and many healthy years past retirement age. They can be encouraged to put their talents to good use for others and to become active collaborators in caring for those who are infirm, elderly, or who just need a friend.

Concern for the Environment

Reverence for God is reflected in reverence for all of God's creation. The issues of pollution, protection of endangered animal species, and the proper disposal of waste and chemicals is ultimately a religious issue. Since all people are called to protect creation and be stewards of God's manifold gifts, no one religious community on its own can address this problem. Interfaith cooperation is necessary to promote workable public policy and to educate people to live in better harmony with the environment.

Youth Programs

While certain youth activities are best kept within the local congregation, other events like sports and recreational programs, social groups and scouting, and spiritual activities which avoid aggressive proselytizing might be appropriate areas for ecumenical activity. Young people need to be encouraged to make ecumenical and interreligious activity a priority in their lives. When adult members of religious communities are actively engaged in ecumenical and interfaith activity, youth activity will be appropriate and feasible.

Promoting Morality

Sometimes there is a fine line separating strictly religious issues from issues of civic morality. Religious groups have an obligation to teach the truth regarding public and private morality and to call individuals to strive for their highest human potential. It is the responsibility of every religious person to make the community a fit place in which to live and to raise children, a place which reflects religious ideals and beliefs.

Pornography

People of all faiths have an obligation to hold their merchants accountable for what is sold in their neighborhood stores. Churches and religious groups ought to petition national networks and local cable networks to provide suitable, healthy, moral programming. Parents ought to carefully monitor what their children watch and act together to address their concerns to national television and radio companies. *Morality in Media* is just one organization that can help to bring many separate concerns together in one voice.

Substance Abuse

In a culture awash in drug and alcohol abuse, it is important for ecumenical and interfaith groups to directly combat this scourge. Alcoholics Anonymous, Alanon, Alateen, and similar groups are always looking for places to meet and help those facing alcohol and drug dependency. Religious leaders ought to pool their resources whenever possible and make space available for such groups to meet so that every person in the community has access to help. In addition, drug and alcohol education programs may best be offered in churches where supportive spiritual communities already exist.

Abortion and Pro-life Issues

Since 1973, more than one-and-a-half million babies have been aborted *each year.* Increasing numbers of religious groups are condemning the taking of unborn life. Ecumenical support groups such as *Women Exploited by Abortion* and *Project Rachel* for women who have been scarred physically and emotionally by abortion need the support of all faiths. Political action groups like the National Right to Life Committee also need broad religious support.

Other pro-life issues related to world peace, world hunger, capital punishment, and political oppression merit broad ecumenical and interreligious support. Respect for life in all forms has to be at the core of the spiritual and moral values of every human being. Individual congregations and local ecumenical groups can serve to educate their members to these issues and mobilize them to act in appropriate ways to petition legislators to enact pro-life legislation.

Other Areas of Concern

The areas recommended in this chapter for ecumenical concern do not exhaust the list of possibilities. New areas of moral concern arise with each new social change. There are other concerns that will affect a particular locale. What needs to be remembered is that each of these concerns can be a reason for ecumenical activity and growth.

Conclusion: That All May Be One

Hopefully this book will help people of goodwill to practice their faith and to exercise their love for God and neighbor in a culture as diverse and pluralistic as that of America. As global communication becomes more efficient, the destiny of the human family becomes more focused, more united. World cultures and economies are more interdependent than ever before. Interfaith understanding needs to keep pace.

The Second Vatican Council has challenged Catholics to deal creatively and constructively with members of other religions and other Christian communities. Catholics are asked to promote reconciliation among other Christians in the same way they are to promote reconciliation between the individual person and Christ. The Catholic Church has mandated that ecumenical and interfaith relationships consciously be fostered by all Catholics. Utilizing the information and suggestions found in this book may help all people cooperate more fully with God's grace. Ecumenical and interfaith relationships have a central place in further establishing the kingdom of God which Jesus Christ inaugurated. Christian unity and greater understanding among members of world religions are not pious wishes; they are Christ's mandates. He promises to bless any and all legitimate efforts toward those ends.

Other helpful books . . .

HOW TO SURVIVE BEING MARRIED TO A CATHOLIC
In 64 colorful, interesting pages, this book gives clear and honest answers to many questions asked by partners in interfaith marriages. It illustrates the central beliefs of Catholics using a lively cartoon format along with pages of text. **$3.95**

THE ILLUSTRATED CATECHISM
Catholic Belief in Words and Pictures
Using a basic question-and-answer format along with over 250 illustrations, this book uses the latest educational methods to introduce today's generations to the teachings of the Catholic Church. **$4.95.** **Leader's Guide $4.95**

THE CATHOLIC CHURCH STORY
This popular, easy-to-read history shows the tremendous impact the Catholic Church has had on the formation of world history over the past 2,000 years.
$4.95. **Leader's Guide $2.95**

CATHOLIC ANSWERS TO FUNDAMENTALISTS' QUESTIONS
This book, written for Catholics as well as questioning Fundamentalists, offers clear, accurate answers to a great many questions sincere Christians ask about the Catholic Church. **$1.95.** **Spanish edition $2.50**

Order from your local bookstore or write to:
Liguori Publications, Box 060, Liguori, Missouri 63057-9999
(Please add $1.00 for postage and handling for orders under $5.00; $1.50 for orders over $5.00.)